Traveler and the Chaplain

A Christian Parable

by Kurt Bennett

Copyright © 2009 by Kurt Bennett. All rights reserved.

Second Edition Copyright © 2014 by Kurt Bennett. All rights reserved.

Unless otherwise noted, scripture references are from the New International Version of the Bible.

Second Edition

Published by Enoch Media, 11875 SW Lynnridge Ave., Portland, OR 97225
kurt@kurtbennettbooks.com

Acknowledgments

It's been said that the best way to succeed is to fail as fast as possible. If that's true, then the second best way to succeed is to watch someone else fail as fast as possible. Watching someone else fail is a kind of rehearsal for the problems you face in your own life. This book provides a close up observation of someone doing just that, someone failing fast.

I am indebted to my family and all the fire department personnel who endured through my failures. God used each of them to teach me about leadership.

For reviewing this work and making recommendations, I want to thank my beautiful wife Kathy, my two sons Gabriel and Nathaniel (arrows in my quiver), my two daughters Charise and Anastasia, my earthly father and mothers, my sisters Kim, Karla, and Jessica, Steve Lumpp, Patricia Lumpp, my good friends Gary Montgomery, Keith and Suzy Kuhl, Bruce Hoy, Andrea Gamble, Gordon Sletmoe, Greg Kleinberg, Kevin Sherry, Carey Auwarter-Sherry, Rodney Pierson, Trevor Hill, Rick Chown, Bob and Janice Thornley, my own fire department chaplain John Minor, and my pastor Jon Courson.

Most of all I am indebted to Jesus Christ, the one who saved me, and the greatest leader of all.

Contents

1. The Chaplain
2. Me, A Leader?
3. What Traveler's Wife Grace Did at 10:45 PM
4. Grace at 11:45 PM
5. Influence
6. Grace at 12:45 AM
7. The Greatest of These is Love
8. Traveler Confronts Grace
9. Humility
10. Grace at 1:45 AM
11. Passion
12. Is Anything Really a Secret?
13. Fruit and the Finer Points
14. Grace Face to Face With Her Past
15. Example
16. The Last Visit
17. The Master
18. Notes

Traveler and the Chaplain/10

The Chaplain

In the beginning...
-John 1:1

An ordinary young man joined the army. In the course of his career he made more than his share of mistakes, but he managed to learn from his mistakes. And though he had no extraordinary qualities, he somehow managed to become a Special Forces leader. After many successful years in the army, progressing through the ranks, he retired. A devout Christian, he moved to an average town where he studied to become a pastor. After completing his studies, he started a church. His idea was to pastor a small church but, somehow, the church grew to 7,000 members. When the military base in town learned he had a background in the army, they asked him, and he agreed, to become their Chaplain.

But this story is not about the army or the Special Forces. It's not about the Chaplain's church. It's not even about the Chaplain, really.

This story is about a young man named Traveler, who happened to live in the same average town.

Your Story

1.   In your own experience, who would you say is the best leader you have ever known? Who is your role model?

Traveler and the Chaplain/13

Me, A Leader?

When they arrived, Samuel saw Eliab and thought, "Surely the LORD's anointed stands here before the LORD."
-1 Samuel 16:6

Traveler was just a regular guy, with a regular family, and a regular job. Lately he had begun to doubt his ability to function at work, and even as a husband and father. His confidence hit bottom somewhere around the time he had a disagreement with his daughter Hope, about a spring break trip to an out of town resort.

"Daddy, but why?" Hope said, near tears.

"I just don't think it's a good idea for you and your friend, two thirteen year-old girls, to go to the resort over spring break. Not without an adult," Traveler said.

"Her older sister will be with us and she's

nineteen. That means she's an adult dad!"

"Nineteen is not old enough," Traveler said.

"You're ridiculous! You're treating me like a little girl!" The tears were starting to flow now.

"She does have a point," Traveler's wife Grace said. "You can't treat her like a little girl forever."

"You can't be serious!" Traveler said. "You don't actually agree with her, do you?"

"I just think the girls come from a nice family," Grace said. "The resort is a nice place. Maybe we should let her go."

"Unbelievable! No, there's no way. She's not going."

Hope cried out, "You're pathetic!" as she ran from the room.

Grace turned her back, and walked away. She began cleaning in the kitchen with enough noise and "enthusiasm" to make sure Traveler knew her frustration.

The next day at work, Traveler found out he didn't get the promotion to the supervisor position he had been seeking. In fact, a less experienced candidate who was below him on the eligibility list was promoted in his place. This was the second time he had been passed over in this manner. He sensed that most of his coworkers agreed with the boss's decision. And as though providence were rubbing it in, the newly promoted supervisor was assigned to manage

Traveler's department. He would be supervised by his rival. When he found out about being passed over and who his new boss would be, he struggled with his emotions. He felt frustrated, embarrassed, inadequate.

His managers told Traveler, he would remain at the top of the candidate list, to be used as a fill in for other supervisors when they took time off.

After work, still feeling down and desperate, he shared the news with Grace. She didn't have much to say. She was still upset with him from the night before. Traveler needed to talk to somebody, so he phoned a friend. After listening to Traveler for a few minutes, Traveler's confidant, who was a soldier, recommended Traveler speak with the army Chaplain. Traveler, who wasn't a soldier, felt awkward about it.

"It won't matter that you're not a soldier. He's a great man. Everyone in my unit loves the guy. My Lieutenant raves about him. Just talk to him. You'll see," Traveler's friend said.

"I don't know..."

"Listen, this guy is not your typical Chaplain. When he was young he led a Special Forces unit."

"Really?"

"Yes, and then he promoted up through the ranks..." Traveler's friend went on to describe the Chaplain's background. Traveler had to confess he sounded interesting, and decided to give him a try. He made an appointment, and a few days later he found himself in the Chaplain's office.

Traveler didn't know what a Special Forces leader was supposed to look like, but he was sure this man did not look like one. The Chaplain was just finishing up what appeared to be a small remodel job in a room next to his office. He was average looking. With his jeans and his tool belt, he could have passed for a carpenter.

"Traveler, come in! I understand you have some questions about life and leadership," the Chaplain said warmly as he removed his tool belt from around his waist. "How can I help you?"

"You can help me find a way out of this supervisor thing. I haven't promoted yet, but I'm still a candidate for a leadership position at work, and I just need a graceful way out. I want to withdraw my name from the candidate list."

"Why do you say that?"

"Because my wife doubts me, my daughter doubts me, my coworkers doubt me, my boss doubts me. I just need a way out. You know, an exit strategy."

"H'mmm, I see," the Chaplain paused for a long moment, lost in thought. Then he said, "Traveler, close your eyes, and tell me what you see when you hear the word 'leader.'"

"Huh?"

"Please, indulge me."

"Alright," Traveler closed his eyes, and took a

deep breath. "I see a man around fifty years old or so. He's tall and handsome. He carries himself well. Uh, he has a grace about him. He's charismatic and well spoken. He has a baritone voice. He's intelligent but not too nerdy or geeky. He has a dignity about him. And he's dressed for success. How's that?"

"Wow, that's more than I bargained for," the Chaplain said smiling.

"Well yes, but you have to understand, I'm none of those things," Traveler said.

"Traveler, a number of years ago two men, Warren Bennis and Burt Nanus, set out to find what a successful leader looked like. They studied ninety of the most outstanding leaders of our time. The list included Ray Kroc, the man responsible for the success of McDonald's; Donald Seibert, chairman of the board of JC Penney; John Robinson, former coach of the USC Trojans and the Rams football teams; and Neil Armstrong, the first man on the moon. Are you getting the picture?"

"I think so. They studied ninety of the most prominent leaders they could find."

"Right. All ninety were surveyed. Some were even shadowed, that is Bennis and Nanus were allowed to follow them around for a few weeks. Two of these leaders actually allowed Bennis and Nanus to live with them for a period of time. Now Psalm 75 says,

> ...*promotion cometh neither from the east, nor from the west, nor from the south. But God is the judge: he putteth down one, and setteth up another.*[1]

"In other words, God chooses who will lead. It follows then that the research done by Warren Bennis and Burt Nanus will show us just what type of person God chooses to put into leadership. Wouldn't you agree?"

"I think I see what you mean," Traveler answered. "If God decides who will be a leader, and if Bennis and Nanus studied ninety of the most prominent leaders of our time, then it follows we'll find out what type of person God chooses to lead."

"Exactly!" the Chaplain responded. "And from their research, what we discover is, when it comes to who will lead, God has narrowed it down to the following types of people: 'Right-brain dominant and left-brain dominant, tall and short, fat and thin, articulate and inarticulate, assertive and reserved, dressed for success and dressed for failure...'[2] In other words, outwardly, leaders come in all shapes and sizes. Just because you don't match up well with the charismatic good looking hypothetical leader you described earlier, in no way implies you're not cut out for leadership."

Traveler leaned forward slightly in his chair.

The Chaplain continued, "1 Samuel chapter 16 describes when Samuel came to Jesse's family to anoint the next king of Israel. It says,

> *When they arrived, Samuel saw Eliab and thought, "Surely the LORD's anointed stands here before the LORD." But the LORD said to Samuel, "Do not consider his appearance or his height, for I have rejected him. The LORD does not look at the things man looks at. Man looks at the outward appearance, but the LORD looks at the heart." …Jesse had seven of his sons pass before Samuel, but Samuel said to him, "The LORD has not chosen these." So he asked Jesse, "Are these all the sons you have?"*[3]

The Chaplain said, "As a leader, David wasn't on anyone's radar, except the Lord's! Not even his own father thought of him as a potential leader. Apparently David didn't look like a leader. He didn't fit man's idea of what a leader should be."

"Okay, but that's only one scripture," Traveler said.

The Chaplain answered, "Other scriptures also point toward those who doubted David. When David was inquiring about Goliath, David's oldest brother Eliab scoffed at David. Eliab said,

> *Why have you come down here? And with whom did you leave those few sheep in the desert? I know how conceited you are and how wicked your heart is; you came down only to watch the battle.*[4]

"His own brother!" The Chaplain said. "Later we see King Saul also doubts David when he said,

> *You are not able to go out against this Philistine and fight him; you are only a boy, and he has been a fighting man from his youth.*[5]

"And David is doubted again by Goliath:

> *He looked David over and saw that he was only a boy, ruddy and handsome, and he despised him.*"[6]

Still not convinced, Traveler said, "Okay, but that's just David, just one person from the Bible…"

The Chaplain interjected, "Throughout the scriptures we find many who were chosen by God to lead, but didn't fit man's image of a leader. Some would say Abraham lacked courage. He told people Sarah was his sister out of fear for his life.[7] Moses was a murderer, and he had a fear of public speaking.[8]

Elisha lacked the look of a leader. Young men mocked his appearance.[9] Isaiah had unclean lips.[10] At Job's low point, everyone, including Job himself, perceived Job as a has-been, washed up.[11] Several verses in the book of Joshua indicate Joshua lacked courage…"[12]

Traveler tried to interrupt, "Alright, I think I…"

Ignoring Traveler, the Chaplain continued in almost rapid-fire fashion, "Paul lacked political capital after persecuting Christians.[13] Peter was too impulsive. He rebuked Jesus when Jesus was talking to Peter about what the Messiah must suffer.[14] And of course many of Peter's contemporaries would probably have said he lacked commitment, because he denied Christ.[15] Solomon was the son of an adulteress.[16] Timothy was too young…"[17]

"Okay! I get it," Traveler interrupted.

The Chaplain paused for a moment, then said, "Being doubted is a normal part of life for those who are chosen to lead by God. Humanity's idea of what a leader is, even your own idea of what a leader is, is not the same as God's idea."

"Alright, then what *are* the keys to leadership?" Traveler asked.

"Well the first and most important key is influence."

"Influence? What do you mean by that, exactly?"

"Let me pray about what is meant by that, exactly. Come back next week, and I'll give you an answer."

Traveler agreed to come back the next week.

Now that he knew experiencing doubt from others is a normal part of life for anyone in leadership, Traveler felt a sense of relief. As he drove home he pondered 1 Samuel 16:7…

> *The LORD does not look at the things man looks at. Man looks at the outward appearance, but the LORD looks at the heart.*

Your Story

1. *How have you been criticized recently?*

2. *What's one of the worst criticisms you ever received?*

3. *Do you ever feel that people around you, doubt you?*

4. *How do the doubts and criticisms in your own life compare to those of David's, or other leaders in the Bible?*

What Traveler's Wife Grace Did at 10:45 PM

Traveler's wife Grace grew up an ordinary young woman. She was never pretty or popular in high school or college. But while in college, Grace did meet an ordinary young man. They fell in love and married. Not long after they were married, Grace and her husband Traveler, had a daughter named Hope.

Grace is the kind of woman who gets things done. She volunteers one day a week at her church. She works part time as a medical clerk in an OB-GYN office. . She loves her daughter and does everything she can to be the best mother she can be. She loves her husband too. But recently he's been consumed with work. So much so, she told a friend the other day, she sees the mailman more than she sees her husband. Even when he's home, his mind is at work. He's always staring into his laptop, or texting on his phone, or emailing, or taking a phone call—for work. He was, for all practical purposes, absent from Grace's life.

And tonight Grace's husband was in bed early--as usual. Grace was wide awake. She was on her laptop, browsing her social network, when a request popped up:

Connection Request—Ethan Arnold, 17 mutual connections. Accept or Deny?

Grace chose to Accept.

Your Story

1. *Talk about a time when you struggled with balance in your life.* -1796733941.

Grace at 11:45 PM

One week after the connection request, at 11:45 PM. On Grace's social network:

Direct Message from Ethan Arnold: Hi, do you remember me? We dated a few times in high school. You used to help me with my assignments in English.

Grace: Of course I remember you Ethan. How have you been?

Ethan: Great. How about you? Are you married? Do you have any kids?

Grace: Yes, married for fourteen years. One daughter. How about you?

Ethan: Was married. We're separated. No kids.

Grace: Sorry to hear that.

Ethan: Don't be, it was probably best.

Grace: It's so great to hear from you. What do you hear from the old crowd...?

Your Story

1. *Do you think you invest in your relationship with Christ as much as he would like?*

2. *If you're married, do you think you invest in your relationship with your spouse as much as God would have you to? Your kids?*

Influence

> *When they saw the courage of
> Peter and John and realized that they
> were unschooled, ordinary men,
> they were astonished and they took note
> that these men had been with Jesus.*
> -Acts 4:13

That week Traveler began to notice Grace was spending more and more time on her laptop and phone. While they normally went to bed together, lately Grace was coming to bed rather late, after Traveler had already retired. He couldn't remember exactly when it started, maybe two or three weeks ago? The way they were getting along lately, he couldn't help but wonder if she was chatting with someone, maybe even a male friend. Sometimes it seemed she was trying to keep him from seeing the screen of her laptop. For this reason, he was distracted the day of his appointment with the Chaplain and almost forgot about it.

He walked in ten minutes late.

"Traveler, how good to see you again," the Chaplain said, smiling broadly.

Traveler mumbled, "Good to see you too."

"Are you okay?" the Chaplain asked.

"Yes, I'm fine. I mean, no, not really."

"Is there anything I can do to help?"

"No. I don't think so."

"Would you like to talk about it?"

"Well…" Traveler hesitated. "It's just that my wife Grace is spending quite a bit of time online lately. Usually it's late at night, I mean like, really late, sometimes until midnight. It just makes me wonder… if… I don't know."

"Are you wondering about the possibility she's in a relationship online?" the Chaplain asked.

"Well, you know, I hear about that sort of thing all the time," Traveler said.

"Can I pray for you?"

"Sure."

The Chaplain prayed for Traveler's wife Grace. He prayed for strength and wisdom for Traveler. He prayed for Traveler and Grace's marriage. And he prayed for God's Spirit to be upon their meeting.

Afterwards he said, "I think what we'll be talking about today may help you with your situation. Shall we get to it?" the Chaplain asked.

"Yes, I guess so." Traveler said.

"Tell me Traveler: What is leadership? How would you define it?"

"I don't know. To tell you the truth, I haven't given it much thought."

"H'mm," the Chaplain thought for a moment.

"Well, are you going to tell me?" Traveler asked.

"Oh yes, of course. Leadership is influence."

"Leadership is influence? That's it? You said you were going to tell me the most important key to leadership. And you said it might help with my marriage. Is that it?" Traveler asked.

"Let me explain," the Chaplain answered. "Let's suppose for a minute you're interested in becoming skilled at making money."

Traveler, obviously interested, straightened slightly in his seat, "Who isn't?"

The Chaplain looked mildly surprised at Traveler's response as he continued, "What would you say if I told you I could provide you with access to one of the richest men in the world?"

"Where do I sign up?" Traveler asked, obviously interested.

The Chaplain said, "The man I'm talking about is Warren Buffett. His net worth is estimated at 418,000 times that of the average person's in the United States. He's widely regarded as one of the greatest financial minds in the world today. What if I could arrange for you to have dinner with him, go for a long walk, have a cup of coffee? You could spend time with him any way you chose. All the while asking any questions of him you wished. If I could arrange it, what would you do?"

"I'd jump at the chance! One or two stock picks from Warren Buffett and you might be set for life, at least financially."

The Chaplain said, "That may well be true. If you spent enough time with Buffett, it's likely your ability to steward the Lord's blessings would improve radically. Now, what if I told you I could provide you access to a leader far greater than Warren Buffett? As wise and talented as Buffett is in the arena of finances, his wisdom and leadership abilities pale in comparison to this person's."

Traveler was excited, "Yes, I mean, could you? Can you?"

"Yes I can."

"Who is it?"

"Jesus Christ."

"Jesus Christ? I don't understand."

"Listen carefully. I define leadership with one word: influence.[1] And Jesus is by far the most influential person in history."

Traveler stared looking somewhat bewildered.

"What's the matter?" The Chaplain asked.

"Well, I'm a little embarrassed to say it to a pastor, or, I mean, a chaplain, uh, I suppose you're both. But it's just I never really thought of Jesus in that way. Do you know what I mean?"

"Sure, yes, I understand. Let me see if I can explain it further. During Jesus' time on earth his influence on his immediate followers is obvious. Just look at how they died: Matthew was run through with a sword. Mark was killed by dragging him behind horses. Luke was hanged. Peter was crucified upside down. Bartholomew was beaten to death. Andrew crucified. Thomas stabbed. All of these men were influenced to the point of giving their lives for Jesus' sake."[2]

The Chaplain was becoming more and more animated as he continued. "And thousands of years later Jesus is still by far the most influential person who ever lived. The Bible is the best selling book in history. Every college established in colonial America (except for one) was created by a denomination of Christianity. Colleges like Harvard, Princeton, Dartmouth, and Yale. The first hospital in history was established by Jesus' followers in 369 A.D. Today, Jesus' church is the largest single provider of healthcare in history. If you ever wondered why so many of our hospitals are named after Christian saints: Saint John's, Saint Jude's, Saint Peter's, now you know. The church established the first orphanage in history, and has the largest orphanage system in the world. During the time of the Roman Empire it was common for people to kill their female babies. But it was Christ's influence, through his followers, that changed the Roman culture to eliminate infanticide. Christian abolitionists influenced the United States to eliminate slavery. The door of time itself is hinged on the life of Jesus Christ. Our dating system is of course divided by B.C., Before Christ, and A.D., Anno Domini, after Christ's birth.[2]

Traveler sat listening wide eyed.

The Chaplain said, "The great historian Will Durant wrote: 'Caesar hoped to reform men by changing institutions and laws; Christ wished to remake institutions, and lessen laws by changing men.' Some leaders focus their efforts on changing organizational structure, or developing rules. Jesus' style is to influence people. And no one in history has influenced people more."[3]

"I never thought of Jesus in that way," Traveler said.

The Chaplain continued, "And unlike Warren Buffett, you, as a Christian, have access to Christ. You can spend time with Jesus when you read your Bible, when you pray, when you take communion, when you spend time in church, when you fellowship with other Christians, when you sing praise songs or hymns, when you fast unto the Lord, and when you meditate on the Bible. By far the most important key to leadership, the most important thing you can do to become a better leader, a better father, a better husband, a better Christian is to be changed like Peter and John were changed, through spending time with Jesus Christ."

"Wait. Changed like Peter and John?" Traveler asked.

"Yes," the Chaplain said. "Shortly after Jesus ascended to heaven, Peter and John had to appear before the rulers, elders, and teachers of the law. The biblical record says,

> *When they saw the courage of Peter and John and realized that they were unschooled, ordinary men, they were astonished and they took note that these men had been with Jesus.*[4]

"Peter and John were changed because they had been with Jesus. They were unschooled ordinary men, yet they demonstrated such courage, and represented Jesus so impressively, they astonished the authorities in Israel. They went on to become great leaders in the early church. You can have a similar life changing experience."

"Me?"

"Yes. Simply recognize leadership is influence, and before you influence others, you must first be influenced by Jesus Christ yourself."

Traveler sat back in his chair, taking it all in. He was quiet for a long time. Then he asked, "So that's the most important key to leadership, but is there more?"

"If you never learn another thing from me, beyond what you learned today, you would be in good stead. But let me pray about your question for awhile. Come back in a month and I'll give you an answer."

"So what about my wife Grace, and her late night social network thing?"

"Have you talked with her about it yet?"

"No."

"I think you'll find some answers in Jesus Christ," the Chaplain said. Paul told the church in Corinth to, 'Follow my example, as I follow the example of Christ.'[5] By far, the most impactful thing you can do to improve any relationship is to become as much like Christ as you can. That being said, you probably need to ask her about it. Just see what she says."

Traveler felt conflicted. Part of him wanted so badly to do just that, to ask her directly what she was doing on the internet so late into the night. But another part of him wanted to believe what she was doing was innocent. He wanted to trust her. Traveler didn't respond to the Chaplain's suggestion.

The Chaplain continued, "How about if you study Jesus over the next month, and then talk to me about Grace when you return?"

Traveler forced a smile and said, "Alright, I'll

see you in a month."

On the way home that evening Traveler pondered what the Chaplain had said, "Before we influence others, we must first be influenced by Jesus ourselves."

And he considered the scripture,

> *When they saw the courage of Peter and John and realized that they were unschooled, ordinary men, they were astonished and they took note that these men had been with Jesus.*[4]

Your Story

1. *Who has the most influence on you in your own life?*

2. *If you had to choose between learning from Warren Buffett how to become rich financially, or learning from Jesus Christ how to become rich in your relationship with God, which would you choose?*

3. *What are you doing to draw closer to Christ?*

Grace at 12:45 AM

Grace one month after her last chat with Ethan Arnold, at 12:45 AM. On Grace's social network:

Ethan: I was looking at some of your photos online today. You look great. I mean, you and your family look great.

Grace thought to herself, "Are you serious? I don't think I look great. I never thought of myself as pretty. And I was never popular growing up." But she typed, "That's sweet of you to say, but I'm older now."

Ethan: No seriously, you look great!

Embarrassed, Grace couldn't think of anything to type.

Ethan: You look like you have a good marriage. You're lucky. My marriage—not so great.

Grace: Photos don't always tell the story, I guess every marriage has issues.

Ethan: Really? You look so happy in your photo albums.

Grace: I know, but my husband, he's good in some ways, but he has some problems.

Ethan: I'm sorry to hear that. If you ever need to talk, I'm a good listener.

Grace: Hmmm.

Ethan: Try me.

Grace: Well… our problem, or his problem is… Like a month or so ago our daughter wanted to go on this really neat little vacation with a friend. Both Hope and I—that's her name, my daughter's name, Hope—we both thought it would be great, but he wouldn't let her go.

Ethan: My ex could be like that. She ruled with an iron fist.

Grace: Exactly!

Ethan: It was her way—or I'd pay.

Grace: Yes! That's how he is too. At least sometimes. Lately he's all about work. He can be so selfish…"

<u>Your Story</u>

1.   If you're married, do you think your spouse feels like you're completely available to talk about their problems?

2.   When was the last time you brought your problems to God in prayer?

The Greatest of These is Love

*If I... have not love,
I am only a resounding gong
or a clanging cymbal.*
-1 Corinthians 13:1

During the next month Traveler received some unexpected news. A supervisor was retiring on short notice.

"Back problems. He's going out on a disability." The Human Resources Director had said. "Traveler, we'd like you to take his position."

Traveler was ecstatic. He immediately called home and shared the news with Grace. However, later in the day his enthusiasm was dampened when he saw the memo outlining transfers created by the retirement and promotion. An assistant manager named Abner was assigned to work for Traveler.

Ab had quite a reputation as a difficult person.

After just a few weeks, Ab was living up to that reputation. He butted heads with Traveler, challenging him on everything from scheduling decisions to supply orders. Although it helped to keep in mind, all God's leaders deal with doubt, still, Traveler felt he should be doing something more to help the situation, but he didn't know what.

Almost a month after his promotion something happened to further complicate things. The ringing telephone woke him late in the night.

"Hello?" Traveler croaked.

"Traveler, it's Ab."

"Oh, Ab, what's going on?" The words came sluggishly as Traveler struggled to clear his sleepy mind.

"My daughter had an accident."

"I'm sorry. Is she okay?"

"No, she's not. She's gone. She died." Strangely, Ab didn't sound sorrowful but had the same familiar abrasive edge to his voice Traveler heard every day at work.

He didn't know what to say. He vaguely recalled in a situation like this you should try to listen. So for the next twenty minutes or so, Traveler did his best to be a good listener. He heard all the details concerning the accident. And he learned how much time off Ab would require.

At the end of the conversation Traveler asked Ab if there was anything he could do for him. But Ab replied, "Thanks but I have everything taken care of."

After Traveler hung up, he was left with the troubling sensation Ab had not responded to him well. He couldn't help feeling as though he hadn't done enough.

The next morning he met with the Chaplain for the third time. Traveler looked distraught.

"Everything okay?" the Chaplain asked.

Traveler was still troubled by his wife's late night social network habits. The other day, on his way to the kitchen, he noticed a man's name he didn't recognize, on the screen of her laptop. Part of him was tempted to wait until Grace wasn't around and then dig through her social network account, email, and text messages, but so far he had opted not to. He thought about broaching the topic with the Chaplain, but instead decided Ab's daughter's car accident was more pressing.

Traveler responded to the Chaplain's question, "Is everything okay? Well, no actually. I have a problem, or problems. Since I saw you last, a great deal has happened. I was finally promoted to the supervisor's position I wanted."

"Well congratulations! I'm not surprised. Traveler. I believe the Lord is going to accomplish great things through your leadership," the Chaplain said smiling.

"The thing is," Traveler said, "there's this guy at work named Ab, and he has a reputation. He's abrasive, and rebellious, and... just difficult to handle. He's an assistant supervisor, and right after I was promoted he was transferred to my department. It wasn't long before he was butting heads with me..."

The Chaplain interrupted, "What are Ab's good qualities?"

Traveler thought for a moment, "Well, I have to admit he is very passionate about making our company the best we can be." He thought a moment more. "And he's a very hard worker. And it seems like he genuinely cares about the people he's responsible for. Yeah, I have to admit, he has some good qualities."

The Chaplain, with a look of satisfaction on his face, said, "I'm sorry, I interrupted. Please go on."

"Well, late last night he called me and told me some terrible news. His teenage daughter died in a car accident. She was a passenger. They think the driver may have been drinking."

Traveler paused.

"Go on." The Chaplain prompted.

"Well, since we last talked I've been trying to spend time with Jesus like you said, you know, reading scripture, praying, church... I can't exactly explain it but somehow I think my time with Him has made me feel I should do something more for Ab. The thing is, I don't know what. I asked Ab if I could do anything for him, but in typical Ab fashion he said he had everything under control."

"I can't imagine what it's like to lose your child," the Chaplain said sympathetically. He paused then said, "In a way, this makes sense. While I was in prayer over the last month, I felt led by the Holy Spirit to share with you today about love."

The Chaplain paused waiting for Traveler to comment. But Traveler, somewhat overcome with emotion, replied with a blank stare.

The Chaplain said, "Traveler, I want you to look at this as an opportunity."

"An opportunity for what?"

"An opportunity to show Ab the Lord's love. When I was studying to lead my unit in the war, we were required to read an ancient story about a Chinese general named Wu Chi. One of Wu Chi's soldiers was suffering from a battle wound that had abscessed. Wu Chi himself cared for the wound even sucking out the infection. The soldier's mother, hearing this, wailed and lamented. Somebody asked her, 'Why do you cry? Your son is only a common soldier, and yet the commander-in-chief himself has sucked the poison from his sore.' The woman responded, 'Many years ago Lord Wu performed a similar service for my husband, who never left him afterwards… And now that he has done the same for my son, he too will follow Wu I know not where.[1]

"Traveler, it's God's kindness that leads people.[2] I want you to take food over to Ab's house. A lot of food."

"But he said he has everything taken care of," Traveler protested.

The Chaplain answered, "That's what people usually say at a time like this. Trust me. Just do it. Do this, and come back in another month and tell me what happened."

The Chaplain wanted to talk about Grace's internet habits, but they were out of time.

Traveler agreed to take groceries over to Ab as the Chaplain said. A month later he met with him for the fourth time.

"Traveler, how are you?" The Chaplain greeted him with a big smile and a hearty bear hug. Traveler was taken aback by the strength in that hug. It was more powerful than the Chaplain's average looking frame seemed capable of.

"I'm good, thanks," Traveler said. "And thanks for the advice."

"What happened?" the Chaplain asked.

"Well, I took over a few days worth of groceries. Ab was very appreciative. Later he said the food really came in handy. I found out he had a large group of family and friends staying with him around the time of the funeral. It turned out they used every bit of food

I gave them. They also needed someone to watch the house during the funeral service. I didn't realize it, but it's a common practice for thieves to check obituaries and then rob the house of the deceased during the funeral. Anyway, I remembered what you said about the Lord's love, so I offered to watch the house for Ab as well."

"So how have things been going with Ab since the funeral?" the Chaplain asked.

"Well I'll say one thing about Ab, he doesn't bring his problems with him to work. He's been very stoic so far. And there's something else. It's kind of amazing. Ab has been one of my strongest supporters. He's still kind of crusty around the edges, but I have to say, on the whole, he's been, well, an advocate of almost everything I'm trying to accomplish at work. I sort of guess it's because of what I did for him with the food and watching the house. But to tell you the truth, I don't totally understand it."

"Traveler, the difference is, after these events, Ab knows you care about him, he knows you're committed to him, he knows you love him. There's an extremely important principle at work here. The greater your ability to convince your people you genuinely care about them, and are committed to them, and love them, the higher you can set your expectations for those same people."

The Chaplain continued, "Let the people you

lead know you love them. If one of them has suffered an injury, show up at his house and mow the lawn. If one of your people lands in the hospital, pay him a visit. If someone is going through a divorce, take him to lunch and lend him an ear. Part of the answer to the age old question, 'Why do bad things happen to good people?' is when something bad happens, it creates an opportunity for us to share God's love. We need to live out the life of Christ. We need to love people."

Traveler mumbled to himself, "1 Corinthians 13, '...and the greatest of these is love.'"[3]

"Exactly," the Chaplain responded. "Remember too, while difficult times present unique opportunities to show people Christ's love, we have to remain engaged with people all the time. We want to express our commitment and love for people regularly, not just when they're walking in the dark valley. So day in and day out, find ways to respect people, and to provide recognition for people, and to encourage people. Nothing I share with you works without love, and love requires regular ongoing engagement. Jesus engaged to the point he lived with his disciples for three years. His engagement with his followers was amazing: He delivered Holy Spirit inspired teachings, he healed people, he touched people.
He loved people."

The Chaplain continued, "Of course as the

ultimate leader, Jesus provides the ultimate example for us. People are so willing to follow him because he paid the ultimate price. He died for us. He paid for our sins with his blood. There is no question concerning his love for us. And that's one of the reasons Jesus is the greatest leader who ever lived. It's why we're so eager to follow him.

"I'm starting to see," Traveler said, nodding as he soaked it all in. "But the other thing I mentioned before. You know, Grace's late night social network thing. A few meetings ago, you said I'd find answers from studying Jesus, but I'm still troubled by her new habit. I'm still not sure..." Traveler's words trailed off.

"Do you feel you gained any insight at all?" the Chaplain asked.

"Well, there is something from 1 Corinthians 13," Traveler said. "You know, the chapter on love. Well I see Jesus as the embodiment of love. And when I study him, I see how he trusted his disciples, in spite of their faults and flaws. 1 Corinthians 13 lists the attributes of love and one of those attributes is trust. Verse 7 says love always trusts.[4] So I feel like I should trust my wife."

The Chaplain said, "That's an excellent insight Traveler. Whenever, and wherever you can, you should trust, and assume the best in people, and give people the benefit of the doubt, no question. However, I think there are times when it's important to open up a line of communication. I really believe this is one of those times."

The look on Traveler's face said, "But I want to trust her." But he didn't say that. Instead he just smiled and asked, "So what's next?"

"Let me pray about that," the Chaplain said. "Come back in another month, and I'll have an answer for you."

That night Traveler drove home wondering whether or not he should confront his wife Grace about her time on the internet late at night. But he also thought about how his support for Ab made such a dramatic change in their relationship. He thought about the principle the Chaplain shared,

> *The greater your ability to convince your people you genuinely care about them, and are committed to them, and love them, the higher you can set your expectations for those same people.*

He pondered ways in which he could love—like Jesus loved.

Your Story

1. Is the word "love" best described as a verb or a noun?

2. When you talk about other people, do you tend to talk about their strengths, or their shortcomings?

3. Describe an instance when during a time of difficulty someone helped you more than you expected.

4. Describe a time when you helped someone with a difficulty.

5. How can you love people like Jesus loved people?

Traveler Confronts Grace

"I said I would tell you later," Grace said.

"No you didn't. You said you would tell me never," Traveler said, surprised to hear his own voice rising, along with his emotions.

"I did not! You're not listening," Grace said.

"Well, that's what I heard," Traveler said. "Why would you tell me never, or for that matter, why would you tell me later?"

"Look, I just have things to do right now. I have a bunch of stuff to take care of for work tomorrow. That's why I want to talk about it later. Is that too much to ask? Can we talk about this later?"

Traveler was silent.

"It's late," Grace said.

Traveler gave up. She was right, it was late, and they had already been at it for thirty minutes. He had a huge day at work tomorrow and it sounded like Grace did too. But it felt to Traveler like they had been going in circles during the entire conversation.

He went to bed, but sleep did not come easily.

She stayed up--and opened her laptop.

Your Story

1. Have you ever been in an argument at night?

2. Why does the Bible say not to let the sun set on your anger? (Ephesians 4:26)

Humility

*For we do not preach ourselves,
but Jesus Christ as Lord,
and ourselves as your servants for Jesus' sake.
-2 Corinthians 4:5*

Over the next month or so, things at work went very well. As Traveler drew closer to Christ he grew both as a leader of his department and as a man. He decided not to confront Grace any further. He was determined to trust her, in spite of her continued late night forays on the internet. Part of his resolve came from the results he saw as he followed the Chaplain's advice. While it had only been a few months since he was promoted, he could sense he was gradually earning the respect of his people. Things at home were a little better too. There were still occasional disagreements, but as he demonstrated more love and support for his wife and daughter, they were slowly becoming more responsive to him. He felt sure the outlook for his future was improving dramatically. He was gaining confidence. In fact, he became so confident, he canceled his next meeting with the Chaplain. It was around that time he found himself in the middle of a controversy.

A month or so ago a supervisor from another department, named Nick Vandeberg, asked Traveler to take over a project for him. It was an important presentation for one of the company's biggest clients. Nick and Traveler started with the company around the same time and had been friends for years. So when he was asked, Traveler said, "Sure, I'm happy to do it. Only one condition: If I do this for you, you forfeit the right to offer criticism about how I put together this presentation." Both men laughed at the comment. Nick seemed happy to unload all the associated documents he had prepared so far. Traveler was glad he could help out his friend.

A few weeks later it was time for Traveler to do a dry run of the presentation in front of all the members of his, and several other departments. Nick, a few upper management personnel, and the rest of the department supervisors were in attendance.

Traveler was just getting started when Nick interrupted: "These graphics look like they're from a junior high school art class. No kidding. I swear, my son could do a better job, and he's in the eighth grade."

There were a few snickers from around the

room. Traveler had already recognized the problem and planned to improve the graphics before the actual presentation to the client. But he didn't say so. Instead he just thanked Nick for his feedback and continued on with the presentation.

Not more than two minutes later Nick interrupted again: "You're not really going to open with that story are you? I mean, it might be fine for a Sunday school class, but come on."

The room went silent. Traveler was taken aback. Again he thanked Nick for his input, jotted down a note to possibly change his opening anecdote, and then continued.

But just a few minutes more went by and Nick was at it again. The room went silent again. No snickers this time, things were becoming awkward. Traveler was reeling. There was no mistaking it now, this was an obvious attack, from someone he counted as a friend. He felt like his heart and stomach just swapped places.

And so it went for the rest of the presentation. Nick disrupted Traveler's talk every few minutes. As they often did, those from upper management left very early. No one remaining in the room wanted to intervene. It was an impossible situation. Traveler gamely stumbled through the presentation as best he could. When it was over he left quickly.

Later, Traveler talked with Nick about what

happened, but Nick offered no apology and acted as though it was no big deal. Over the next few weeks Traveler offered olive branches by supporting Nick's projects and programs at every opportunity. But nothing seemed to help. From the day of that presentation, his relationship with Nick was never the same.

In fact, through the grapevine, Traveler began to hear rumors of complaints about Traveler's work performance. He couldn't be positive, but he was fairly certain Nick was behind them.

Meanwhile, Nick seemed to be more active than ever, delivering high energy presentations and trainings to all levels of the organization. It seemed as though wherever there was a spotlight to be found, Nick would run underneath it. He obviously enjoyed the attention.

Traveler became increasingly frustrated. He decided to adopt a "what works for Nick Vandeberg can work for me," approach. What was best for his customers, his people, and the company became secondary. "Winning" the battle with Nick became his priority. If there was a high profile assignment, Traveler did his best to acquire it. He started to dress in more expensive clothes. He became more demanding of his people. He even tried to walk with a bit of a swagger. Over a short period of time, he began to look and act less like Traveler, and more like Nick.

These changes were not well received by the personnel in Traveler's department, and Traveler knew it. But he felt if he was going to compete with Nick, the changes were necessary.

As he continued his efforts to imitate Nick, he began to feel more and more uneasy. Traveler decided it was time to visit the Chaplain. Within a few days the two met.

"Traveler, how very good to see you. How have you been?" The Chaplain greeted Traveler.

"Pretty good, mostly. Well, at least until recently," Traveler conceded.

"What's going on?"

"Well, at work there's this guy in another department, he's a supervisor, same as me. And he has a knack for landing the best assignments. He's one of our organization's big contributors."

"H'mm," was all the Chaplain said.

"Let me finish," Traveler said, sounding annoyed. "He's kind of flashy, very high profile. You know, the kind some would call 'a mover and shaker.' We always got along great until I took this presentation project for him. For *him*. I did it as a favor. But then when I presented for practice in front of a large group from the company, he sniped through the whole presentation. I couldn't believe it. It was humiliating."

"Sounds like a sharp guy. What else does he do well?"

Traveler felt his eyes rolling involuntarily, then he recovered his composure and said, "Okay, well, he's a great communicator, and an outstanding salesman, but lately he treats me like he's my boss even though we have the same level of au…"

"Good qualities," the Chaplain interrupted.

"Right," Traveler thought for a moment. "He gives a lot of thought to what's best for the organization. He's highly motivated. He's a great planner."

"I see," said the Chaplain. "Can you think of any reason for his change in behavior?"

"Believe me, I've thought about it quite a bit, and, no, I can't come up with a reason."

"When did it all start?"

"I don't know. A few weeks ago maybe."

"How were things going up until a few weeks ago?"

"Oh, they were going really well!" Traveler's face lit up. "My people were really starting to warm up to me. And my department's performance has been on the increase. We're starting to get noticed. Recently my boss's boss even complimented our performance."

"Biggest dog syndrome," the Chaplain muttered to himself.

"What?" Traveler asked.

The Chaplain said, "Biggest dog syndrome. The other supervisor, he has a case of biggest dog syndrome. When you were a smaller dog, so to speak, everything was fine between you. But now that you've achieved some measure of success, he's uncomfortable. He doesn't mind other dogs in the kennel, as long as he's the biggest.[1] Not that it matters. Tell me this: to what do you attribute your recent success?"

Traveler answered, "All I'm trying to do is spend time with Jesus, learn about him, and show my people and my customers the Lord's love. Oh, and I also try to keep in mind, encountering doubt is a normal part of life for God's leaders. It was really working."

"Was?"

"Yes, was. I guess since this guy has gotten under my skin, I haven't been doing what I should."

The Chaplain said, "It's a life long process Traveler. Spending time with Jesus, learning about him, loving Him, and loving people, the process never ends, ever."

"I guess I know that. I'll need to get back to doing those things. Lately I've been trying to adopt some of Nick's tactics."

"Nick, that's the other supervisor's name?" the Chaplain asked.

Traveler nodded and said, "Nick Vandeberg."

"And you adopted his tactics? What kind of tactics?"

"Oh, just trying to dress a little better. Trying to get the high visibility assignments. I guess I'm also pushing my people to work harder." Traveler sounded a little embarrassed.

"Were they not working hard enough before?"

"They were working plenty hard I suppose, but now I'm trying to outperform his department. Do you have any ideas about what to do with this other supervisor? How can I win this?"

"Who said it's a competition?" the Chaplain asked.

Traveler said, "I'm pretty sure both of us would like to be promoted someday. He'll be one of my rivals, almost certainly."

The Chaplain asked, "Do you remember what we talked about? The verse from Psalm 75?"

"You mean the part about promotion?"

"Yes, that part."

Traveler recited the verse,

> ...promotion cometh neither from the east, nor from the west, nor from the south. But God is the judge: he putteth down one, and setteth up another.[2]

The Chaplain said, "You remember, well done. Traveler, you don't have to worry about the other supervisor. You only have to do your best, and trust God will help you through. It's up to Him," the Chaplain pointed a finger heavenward, "who will be promoted. Before you came over and shared all this with me, do you know what I felt led to talk with you about today?"

"No."

The Chaplain said, "Humility. And sometimes the only way to learn humility is to be humiliated."

Traveler couldn't believe what he was hearing. "Humility? You mean in me? It's the other supervisor who has the problem, not me."

Suddenly a burst of laughter escaped from the Chaplain.

"What's so funny?" Traveler asked. He did his best to sound indignant, but the Chaplain's laughter was infectious.

"Well it's just that… the other supervisor, does he have a problem with humility?"

"Yes. A big problem. His problem is, he doesn't have any."

"And didn't you tell me you've been emulating his tactics lately?"

Traveler paused, then he suddenly looked deflated. "Yes, I guess I did tell you that. When you put it that way… I suppose I haven't been the most humble person lately. I am such an idiot."

Something in Traveler's tone caused the Chaplain to respond quickly and firmly, "Traveler, let's talk a little about what humility is not. Humility is not self-denigration, that is, it's not bitterly berating yourself internally. We need to set high standards for ourselves, and as much as we can, show grace and mercy to those around us. However, when we set those high standards, we need to do it in a way that avoids self-denigration.

When David, his men, and their families were camped at Ziklag they were raided while the men were gone. They lost all they had, including their wives and children. Things were so bad David's men began to talk about stoning him.³ But the Bible says during that time,

> *David encouraged himself in the LORD his God.*⁴

The Chaplain continued, "You need to know it's okay to encourage yourself in the Lord. David did it, and you can read about how he did it in the Psalms. You know that voice in your head? The dialog you have with yourself all the time?"

Traveler answered, "I think so."

The Chaplain said, "The voice that called you an idiot the time you spilled your coffee on the carpet? The voice that called you stupid the time you backed the car into the fence post? The voice that called you a moron the time you overspent the budget?"

"Okay, now I know exactly what you're talking about," Traveler said laughing.

"That internal dialog must be moving you toward excellence, but in a positive way," the Chaplain said. "In the same way David encouraged himself in the Lord, encourage yourself in the Lord."

"I suppose I'm guilty of getting down on myself sometimes," Traveler said.

"Many people mistake self-denigration for humility," the Chaplain said.

"So what is it then? What is humility?" Traveler asked.

"Humility is an absence of pride resulting from a keen awareness of who I am in comparison to God."

Traveler sat with a blank look.

"Let me try to explain," the Chaplain said. "Name one of the most famous athletes in the history of our planet."

"Um, LeBron James?"

"Okay, he played basketball right?"

"Yes. You have to ask?"

Ignoring the question the Chaplain continued, "Suppose you and a friend were playing basketball together on the same team as LeBron James. And at the end of the game the three of you combined for fifty points: you scored one, your friend scored two, and Lebron scored forty-seven."

"That sounds about right," Traveler said.

The Chaplain said, "How ridiculous would it be for your friend to then deride you for not scoring as many points as he? It was LeBron James who scored nearly all the points."

"I guess that would be pretty silly," Traveler said.

"How much greater is the difference between man and God than the difference between your friend and LeBron James?" the Chaplain asked.

"The difference is infinite?" Traveler answered, half asking.

"Yes, that's right! The difference is infinite. Remember the story Jesus told of the Pharisee and the tax collector?"

"Yes."

The Chaplain continued, "Two men went into the temple. The first, a Pharisee, thanked God for making him superior to the other who was a tax collector. The tax collector, recognizing he was a sinner, simply asked God for mercy.[5] Jesus said,

> *I tell you that this man, rather than the other, went home justified before God. For everyone who exalts himself will be humbled, and he who humbles himself will be exalted.*[6]

The Chaplain said, "One of these men, the tax collector, recognized in comparison to God, he was but dust, he was a sinner, he was in need of God's mercy. Pride manifested itself in the other, in the

Pharisee, as he compared himself to another human being. Comparing yourself to another human is ridiculous in the context of God's majesty. We're to esteem all others as higher than ourselves."[7]

"What about outside of the context of God's majesty?" Traveler asked.

"God is ever present, so we're always in the context of His majesty," the Chaplain replied.

"Okay, but didn't the tax collector denigrate himself?" Traveler asked.

"Great question. What the tax collector did was completely appropriate. He humbled himself in the sight of the Lord. I believe that's different than self denigration."

"Be humble Traveler," the Chaplain continued. "Your purpose as a husband, a father, a leader at work is to serve."

"Wait a minute, aren't I the head? The authority?"

"Yes, and your role is to serve. To serve your wife, your daughter, your team at work, your customers. Provide them with what they need to succeed. You're working for them."

Traveler said, "I never thought of it quite that way."

The Chaplain said, "Paul said to those at Corinth,

> ...*we do not preach ourselves, but Jesus Christ as Lord, and ourselves as your servants for Jesus' sake.*[8]

The Chaplain continued, "Remember, Jesus himself washed the disciple's feet."[9]

Traveler and the Chaplain were silent for a long moment. Then Traveler asked, "Okay, but what about this other supervisor, Nick?"

"Just keep doing your job as unto the Lord, and He'll help you through this. You'll see."

"I can do that, I guess. But somehow it doesn't seem like enough. What about ambition? The other supervisor has an abundance of it, and he seems to have all the success."

"Well, you are onto something. That you're ambitious is essential. The greater your ambition, the greater your passion, the greater your success. The question is, what are you ambitious about?"

"What do you mean by that?"

"Let me pray about it. Come back in another two months, and I'll have an answer. Now, what about Grace? Did you talk with her?"

"I did, but it didn't go very well. She didn't want to talk about it. She said it was late and she had some work to do." Traveler said.

"You have to confront her, Traveler."

"But hasn't she earned my trust over the last fourteen years?"

"Look, she's human," the Chaplain said. "Yes she's been trustworthy, but don't you think her avoiding any real discussion about it is an indication she might be doing something you should be made aware of?"

Traveler slowly nodded his agreement.

That night on the way home Traveler thought about what the Chaplain said concerning humility, "Humility is an absence of pride resulting from a keen awareness of who I am in comparison to God."

He also thought about the Chaplain's statement: "Sometimes the only way to learn humility, is to be humiliated."

"Lately it seems," Traveler thought to himself, "God is especially interested that I learn humility."

Your Story

1. Describe a time you felt envious.

2. Describe your inner voice or internal monologue. Is it critical?

3. Read Psalm 56. How did David encourage himself?

4. Describe a leader in your life who lacked humility. How did people respond to him or her?

5. How does God respond to people who lack humility?

6. Do you know someone who looks down their nose at others? Do you know someone who looks down their nose at people who look down their nose at others?

7. What makes the sin of pride so subtle?

Grace at 1:45 AM

After months of chatting online, at 1:45 AM. On Grace's social network.

Ethan: By any chance are you still up?

Grace: Yes, still up. Can't sleep. I've been trying to talk with Traveler for the last three days, but he's all focused in on work.

Ethan: Sorry to hear that. Is there anything I could help you with?

Grace: No, I don't think so.

Ethan: K

Grace: I saw the new pictures you posted in your photo album today. Is that a Harley?

Ethan: Yes, it's brand new—just bought it. I want to

take it over the Rockies to the West Coast. You should come with me.

Grace: Very funny.

Ethan: Why?

Grace: I'm married.

Ethan: So that means you can't take a trip if you want to? I mean, you're an adult right? You can do what you want.

Grace: I could never be gone for that long.

Ethan: What if it was a shorter trip? What if we went up North, just for the day?

Grace: No, a day is too long.

Ethan: How about one hour?

Grace: Hmmmm.

Ethan: Just a one hour ride. You can spare an hour, right? I just need someone I can show it off to.

Your Story

1. *What person in your life do you have the most control over?*

Passion

*Brethren, I do not count myself
to have apprehended; but one thing I do,
forgetting those things which are behind
and reaching forward to those things
which are ahead, I press toward the goal
for the prize of the upward call of God in Christ Jesus.
—Philippians 3:13 (NKJV)*

For the next two months, Traveler renewed his efforts to spend time with Jesus. In addition to attending Sunday service and a mid-week Bible study, he started participating in a morning men's group. At home he became more disciplined in his personal devotional life, and in leading family devotions as well. He did his best to show the Lord's love to his family, his coworkers, and his customers. Traveler made it a point to persistently petition the Lord to remove all pride and to make him precisely as humble as the Lord desired him to be. He sometimes thought it was a dangerous prayer. But as he went deeper and deeper into his relationship with Jesus, his desire to become the most Christlike Traveler he could be, increased. He tried to focus on serving the people he was responsible for. Other than his family and his team at work appearing more comfortable with him, Traveler didn't notice any outward results from the changes he was making. However, inwardly, he did notice Nick's complaints had lost most of their sting. This was surprising since Nick continued his high-energy ascent to stardom. The latest rumor was Nick would receive the next vice president position.

At the end of two months, Traveler met with the Chaplain for the sixth time. "Great to see you, Traveler!" The Chaplain greeted him with a bear hug.

"Great to see you," Traveler replied smiling.

"Tell me how things have been going."

Traveler thought of something that was bothering him. His daughter Hope told him she was concerned about Grace's late night social networking, and that she delved into her laptop one afternoon while Grace was at work. Before she had a chance to share anything more they were interrupted, but Traveler couldn't help but notice the look of worry on Hope's face. That might explain the friction he'd noticed lately between his wife and daughter. Traveler pushed these thoughts to the back of his mind and said, "Things have been fairly calm actually. I've been spending more time with the Lord, and asking Him for humility."

"And how's that been working for you?" the Chaplain asked.

"Well, I haven't seen much of a change in anybody, except my family and my team at work seem to be a little more relaxed around me. There is one interesting thing though."

"What's that?"

Traveler said, "Nick continues to complain about me and my department to anyone who will listen, but it just doesn't seem to bother me as much anymore."

The Chaplain said, "That's because your prayers are being answered."

"How's that?" Traveler asked.

"Have you ever seen someone take an embarrassing fall, then when you asked if they're hurt, they answered, 'Only my pride?'" the Chaplain asked.

"Yes, I suppose I have."

The Chaplain said, "Well if there's no pride inside, then there's no pride to be injured. Humility is a release from pride, and a release from pride is a freeing experience."

Traveler said, "So as God answers my prayers for humility, He removes my pride, and consequently, I'm not so offended."

"Exactly."

"I have to be honest, I was a little apprehensive about praying that way, I thought the answer might be… painful. I didn't expect to enjoy more peace as a result of humility.

"Most people don't recognize humility as a blessing," the Chaplain said.

Traveler said, "I still have a few things about work on my mind. Could we talk about them?"

"Shoot."

"Okay, so his complaints don't really bother me anymore, but I still see the other supervisor doing great things at work. He is so high energy, so loaded with ambition. I'd like to have more of that, more ambition, more passion."

The Chaplain said, "As I said last time we talked, you're on to something when you ask about ambition. Ambition is essential to success as a leader. In fact, I've never seen a successful leader without it."

"Really?"

"Yes. The greater your ambition, the greater your passion, the greater your resolve—the greater your success. The important question to ask though, is, what are you ambitious for?"

"So what's the answer? What should you be ambitious for, as a leader?" Traveler asked. He had been wondering about the answer to this question since his last visit with the Chaplain.

The Chaplain answered, "If I'm hearing you right, the other supervisor, Nick, seems to devote much of himself to selfish ambition. To be a truly great leader, you must be full of ambition for the Lord, and for the organizations he has placed you in: your family, your church, your company, but not for yourself. It's a paradox that one of the great keys to success in leadership is having at your core both passion, and, humility."[1]

"I thought you told me in God's sight there is no set mold for what a leader should be like?" Traveler asked.

"That's true when you're talking about outward things like appearance and charisma," the Chaplain said. "But today we're talking about internal things. God is very interested in the internal part of you, your core. And at your core you must have both great passion, and great humility, to be a great leader."

"I'm not sure I get it," Traveler said. "What about the people I see every day who seek out the limelight? They're the ones who seem to have all the success. Who on earth has both passion and humility?"

"Traveler, have you ever heard of Darwin E. Smith?"

"No."

The Chaplain continued, "How about Colman Mockler, George Cain, Alan Wurtzel, David Maxwell, Jim Herring, Lyle Everingham, Joe Cullman, Fred

Allen, Cork Walgreen, or Carl Reichardt?"

"I haven't heard of any of them. Should I have?"

"Most people haven't, so, no, not necessarily," the Chaplain said. "A man named Jim Collins, he… well I guess you could say he discovered them in a way. Jim wanted to find out what set apart truly great companies from the rest of the pack. So he and his team of researchers identified all the Fortune 500 companies that went from performing below the general stock market average, to outperforming the general market by three times or more. And not only that, but to meet his criteria, they had to sustain that level of performance for fifteen years or more, in a row."[1]

"I think I understand that just well enough to know the bar was set seriously high," Traveler said.

"You're right," said the Chaplain. "In fact, Collins set the bar so high, of the eleven hundred companies that had been in and out of the Fortune 500 during the twenty-five year study period, only eleven met the criteria. The eleven names I mentioned, were the CEOs of those eleven companies."[1]

Traveler couldn't believe it. "Hang on a minute," he said. "You mean to tell me, these eleven people I never heard of before are the cream of the cream? What about guys like Donald Trump?"

"Um, Donald didn't make the list. The reason you've never heard of the eleven is because they weren't concerned with the limelight. Some were even described as shy. All eleven had an absence of selfish ambition. Yet they all had great resolve. They all had that paradoxical combination of passion and humility."

The Chaplain continued, "There's this one story about when the Wall Street Journal tried to interview one of them, Darwin E. Smith, the CEO of Kimberly-Clark. When he asked Smith to describe his leadership style, Smith answered in his characteristic shy and awkard manner with one word, 'Eccentric,' he said. Needless to say, the Wall Street Journal never ran a splashy article on Darwin E. Smith."

"I don't even know what Kimberly-Clark is? What do they do?" Traveler asked.

"Ever hear of Kleenex?" the Chaplain said.

"Yes."

"That's just one of their products. You've been using what they make all your life without even realizing it," the Chaplain said.

He continued, "The great leaders of the Bible all had this unusual combination of passion plus humility. Moses demonstrated great resolve when he confronted Pharaoh again and again and again. He risked annihilation of his people by the Egyptians. And he endured the disobedience and rebellion of his followers. But he never lost his passion for God's directive, for him to lead his people into the promised land.² Moses had great passion *and* he had humility. The Bible says Moses was,

> *a very humble man, more humble than anyone else on the face of the earth.*³

"David slayed Goliath as well as many of Israel's enemies. He persevered through his years as a fugitive running from Saul. He united Israel and Judah into one nation. And he endured a government coup led by his own son. And through it all he never lost his passion for the Lord and for his country. Yet David wrote,

> *Who am I, O Sovereign LORD, and what is my family, that you have brought me this far?*⁵

"David had both great passion and great humility."

"Paul endured plots to kill him, beatings, imprisonment, stoning, riots, and shipwrecks, but did not waver in his passion to spread the gospel. He said,

> *...one thing I do, forgetting those things which are behind and reaching forward to those things which are ahead, I press toward the goal for the prize of the upward call of God in Christ Jesus.*[6]

"Obviously Paul was a passionate man. Yet he also said,

> *For we do not preach ourselves, but Jesus Christ as Lord, and ourselves as your servants for Jesus' sake.*[7]

"Paul thought of himself as a servant: he was humble."

The Chaplain took a breath, "Many have passion without humility. Some have humility without passion. But great leaders have both."

"Passion plus humility," Traveler said to himself. "It seems like Moses, David, and Paul were naturally passionate. I have some motivation for what I do, but I don't feel like I have passion in the same way as the great leaders of the Bible. What can I do to have more passion?"

"Great question Traveler," the Chaplain said. "There are several things you can do. First ask for the empowerment of the Holy Spirit. That's by far the most important."

"So how does asking for the Holy Spirit increase my enthusiasm?" Traveler asked.

The Chaplain said, "The Bible says when the Philistines attacked Samson,

> ...*the Spirit of the Lord came mightily upon him, and the cords that were upon his arms became as flax that was burnt with fire, and his bands loosed from off his hands.*[8]

"Through the empowerment of the Holy Spirit, Samson went on to defeat 1,000 of the enemy—by himself! When you receive the empowerment of the Holy Spirit your passion increases. You said you wanted more enthusiasm?"

"Yes."

"Interesting word. We derive our word enthusiasm from the Greek word en-theos which means *full of God's spirit.*"[9]

"Hmm," Traveler said. He was beginning to understand. "So how do I get it, or Him? The Holy Spirit?"

"You ask God," the Chaplain said.

"I just ask God?"

"Yes. Jesus said,

If you then, though you are evil, know how to give good gifts to your children, how much more will your Father in heaven give the Holy Spirit to those who ask him![10]

"So ask!" The Chaplain said. "Ask God to pour out His Holy spirit upon you. Ask Him for His Holy spirit today. Ask Him for His Holy spirit every day. Ask Him three times a day!"

"Okay, I will." Traveler was smiling, the Chaplain's enthusiasm was irresistible. "I'll ask, persistently. But is there anything else I can do to make myself more passionate?"

The Chaplain said, "Besides asking for the Holy Spirit, spend as much time as you can with passionate people. You do realize you become like those you spend time with, don't you? That's a powerful truth. You must choose very carefully who you keep company with. Choose people who are more passionate, and more godly than you are. That can make a difference."

"Okay, what else?"

The Chaplain said, "You have to leave room for what you desire to be passionate about."

"Huh?"

The Chaplain said, "Okay, so do you remember the last time you stopped for fast food and ate a couple of burgers, some fries, maybe a shake on your way home, and then, when you walk in the door you smell the aroma of a home cooked meal? The kind of home cooked meal with your favorite meat, and gravy, and vegetables, and potatoes, and salad, and dessert, and everything else a great home cooked meal is. It's so completely superior to the fast food you just ate, but, where is your appetite? You can't eat much of what's best, because you've already filled up on what's less. What little you do eat, you don't find enjoyable.

It's the same with life. Don't fill up on the lesser things in life. Leave room for what's important: God, family, work, friends…"

Traveler nodded and said, "Is that it?"

"One last thing," the Chaplain said. "Realize you could be face to face with Jesus Christ at any moment."

"Are you talking about the rapture?" Traveler asked, a little surprised.

"Could be, but regardless of your theological beliefs concerning the rapture, recognize you could die at any moment. I've seen the death of many who were close to me. Some died very young. I pray the Lord will spare you from such a fate, but recognize the simple truth that life is fragile."

Traveler sat quietly, thinking. The Chaplain thought he could almost see Traveler growing as a leader right before his eyes.

As he walked Traveler to the door he said, "You must have passion and humility. As a leader it's essential you have both. And to gain passion, pray for the empowerment of the Holy Spirit, pray often, pray with persistence! Leave room in your heart, and soul, and mind for the Lord and for what He desires you to be passionate about. Spend time with people more passionate and godly than yourself. And finally, realize how fragile life is—you could find yourself standing before Christ this very night."

"Now, what about Grace?" the Chaplain asked.

"I haven't had a chance to talk with her yet," Traveler said. "But I'll do it before our next meeting."

Without another word Traveler walked out the door, lost in thought.

Your Story

1. Who is the most passionate leader you know? Is he humble?

2. Who do you know who is both passionate and humble?

3. When was the most recent time you asked God to give you His Holy Spirit to help you?

4. Who do you know who is more godly and more passionate than you are?

5. Who do you know who died young?

6. Describe a time when you filled up on junk food.

7. What is in your life currently (good or bad) that you could eliminate to make more room for what matters in eternity?

Is Anything Really a Secret?

Grace's sister Charity came into town for a visit one day. Around three o'clock in the afternoon they were together, in Grace's kitchen, alone. After catching up about family, the conversation turned to Grace's new friend.

"So I heard you've been talking with Ethan Arnold," Charity said.

Grace's face flushed. "Why would you say that?"

"I just heard you're trading DMs with him. Prudence (Charity's daughter) mentioned it."

"What's a DM?" Grace asked. "And how would Prudence even know?" As she asked the question, Grace realized the obvious. Her own daughter Hope must have said something to her cousin. "Daddy's girl," Grace thought to herself.

"It's a direct message, a private one, online," Charity answered. "So what do you two talk about?"

"That's none of your business."

"Hey, I'm not judging. There's nothing stopping two adults from having a conversation, right?"

"Yes, that's right. I mean, what have I done wrong?" Grace said. "I haven't done anything to hurt anybody. We're just friends."

"Right, there's nothing wrong with being friends," Charity said.

There was an awkward pause.

"Does Traveler know?" Charity asked.

"I don't know. I'm not trying to hide it from him."

There was another awkward pause. Charity looked down at her phone and excused herself.

Your Story

1. *Do you think it's possible to attack a problem without attacking a person?*

2. *Do you think you could attack a threat to your marriage without attacking your spouse?*

Fruit and the Finer Points

*This is to my Father's glory,
that you bear much fruit,
showing yourselves to be my disciples.
—John 15:8*

Over the next several months Traveler began praying at least once every day for the empowerment of God's Holy Spirit. At times it seemed as though he could feel the presence of God's Spirit upon him. But most of the time he didn't feel any different. He tried to fill up his life with what was most important first, and to avoid spending time on those things without value in God's economy. He started a journal and wrote about what he believed God had in mind for him to accomplish. He also began to pray for God to bring people into his life who were more passionate and more godly than himself.

Around this time he was approached by one of the elders at his church and asked to join the leadership. At his first church leadership meeting, early one Saturday morning, he looked around and realized he was surrounded by men of God who were more passionate and more godly than himself. He was elated! It was an answer to prayer. He began to cultivate friendships with some of the group.

As time passed, Traveler and Grace became more together in parenting styles. And Traveler watched his daughter Hope blossom. She was growing more in Christ each day.

At work Traveler found himself on the receiving end of many requests to lead various projects and programs. As a result of his growing passion he tackled these assignments *heartily, as to the Lord.*[1] Traveler's department flourished even more than before. Traveler felt very much at peace about his life with one nagging exception: the silent tension surrounding Grace's social network addiction.

One Saturday some of the men at the church leadership meeting recommended a few books on leadership. After reading the first of these, Traveler had some questions. He thought it might be a good idea to pay a visit to the Chaplain.

"Traveler, how good to see you. It's been a long time." The Chaplain greeted Traveler with his customary bear hug.

"Good to see you too," Traveler said smiling.

"How is your family? How are things at work?" the Chaplain asked.

"Not without challenges, but both are going well."

"That's good to hear Traveler. So what would you like to talk about today?"

"Well, to start, I was invited to join the leadership at church and…"

"That's great!" The Chaplain interrupted. "That's an honor, to serve your congregation and your community in that way."

"Yes, it is. I'm enjoying it more than I ever thought I would. I have a question though."

"Fire away."

"Some of my new friends have recommended some books on leadership, and I was wondering what you thought of their recommendations."

"I'd be happy to share any thoughts I have, but before we go there, let me ask, are you spending time in God's word?"

"Oh sure, every day. I'm plugged into a men's Bible study on Monday mornings. Grace and I started reading a devotional and praying together every night. I attend our church's midweek Bible study. And of course I go on Sundays. Oh, and I also spend a little time in God's word by myself every morning."

"Excellent," the Chaplain said. "Let me ask you one more thing Traveler, do you realize by reading the Bible, you're already reading the greatest book on leadership ever written?"

"Well, I hadn't thought about it before in those terms, but I see what you mean. Yes, I get it. The Bible is a book about the greatest leader the earth has ever seen."

"Exactly," the Chaplain said. "Now where were we?"

"The books they recommended," Traveler said.

"Right, what books?"

Traveler went on to describe a short list of books on leadership. The Chaplain had read most of them and offered his opinion on each. The Chaplain finished with, "Just be sure to check anything you read with the scriptures to confirm their ideas or principles are consistent with God's."

Traveler asked, "So leadership goes beyond what you and I have talked about here then, doesn't it? I mean, some of these books talk about honesty, building trust, being competent, earning respect…"

"Traveler, those are qualities any Bible believing Christian should have. Wouldn't you agree?"

"Yes, I suppose I do," Traveler answered. "But then what about the finer points? Things like timing, momentum, delegation…"

"There are several good books on the finer

points of leadership. What you and I have been discussing over the last year or so are what I have found to be the essentials. Sometimes it can become difficult to know what to focus on with the huge volume of information available to us today. The essentials of leadership distill down to a deep learning of the life of Jesus, showing people God's love, cultivating those paradoxical and dynamic qualities of passion plus humility, all the while keeping in mind all of God's leaders deal with doubt. There are some others I haven't shared yet. But if you follow these biblical principles, the finer points generally take care of themselves."

"So should I not read books on leadership other than the Bible?"

"I don't think so. I believe that to stop learning is to stop leading.[2] I think it's important to become a lifelong learner. Just be sure to qualify whatever you encounter with the life of Christ. Check it for consistency with God's word."

Traveler nodded his understanding and asked, "May I change the subject? I have a question about communicating ideas and vision."

"Ask away," the Chaplain said.

"As my passion increases, I think I'm getting ideas and vision from the Lord."

"That's great!" the Chaplain said.

"Yes, it is, but sometimes I find it difficult to communicate the vision to my people."

"I see. Casting God's vision and communicating ideas is a very important part of leadership. The most effective leaders I've ever known start by talking to as many key people as they can. Face to face, one on one is best but not always possible. A video chat is next best, then the telephone, then emails and texts messages. You know what else, some successful leaders I know use handwritten notes very effectively. I'm sure you remember how Jesus met face to face with each of his disciples often: sometimes in small groups, sometimes larger groups, and sometimes his disciples were a part of an even larger crowd. The successful leaders I know put in a lot of time meeting with their leadership team and other key people to collaborate on a vision or idea. This enables the leader and his leadership team to finally present his or her vision or idea to the general group with one heart."[3]

"Leadership team?"

"It has to do with fruit. I'm sure we'll get to it shortly," the Chaplain said.

"All those meetings sound like a lot of time and talking…"

"And listening too. Remember, you're not Jesus," the Chaplain said grinning. "God will use the people around you to communicate with you, and to expand your vision. Just like reading leadership books, it's important to filter everything you hear through the scriptures, but start by patiently listening to what people have to say. There's great wisdom within the family of God. After listening, then share the vision God's given you."[4]

"That sounds like a lot of work!" Traveler said.

"True, but that's what it takes to communicate ideas or vision effectively. It's a little easier today with all the different forms of communication we have at our disposal. But even with today's technology, the most common mistake I see is to communicate too infrequently."

"Okay, so what about the other things, your other principles? What are they?" Traveler asked.

"Fruit," the Chaplain answered.

"That's only one."

"I can only talk about one at a time."

"Okay, I'm interested."

"Take a look at 2 Kings chapters 2, 3, and 4." The Chaplain opened his Bible and read the three chapters aloud then said, "Elijah is about to be taken up into heaven. His student Elisha is following him around all day, and in their travels they run into two groups of prophets: one group at Bethel, and another group at Jericho. Here's my question for you, what's going on here with all of these prophets popping up all over Israel?"[5]

"I'm sure you're going to tell me."

The Chaplain became animated and excited, "The prophets are fruit from Elijah's work on earth! They're the result of Elijah's abiding in the Lord, and the Lord abiding in Elijah, and God's words abiding in Elijah. Sometime ago I read a study about elderly people who were about to die. When asked what they would do differently if they could live life over again, they said they would do more things that would last beyond their own passing. Elijah was a great man of God to be sure, but the fruit he left behind accomplished more after his death than Elijah did during his lifetime. Elisha alone performed twice as many miracles as Elijah, not to mention what the other prophets mentored by Elijah may have accomplished."[7]

"So what does that have to do with me?" Traveler asked.

"Disciple your children. Identify future leaders at work and mentor them. Identify leaders at church, and do everything you can to help them grow. Leave behind fruit!"

Traveler said, "So my mission here on earth doesn't end then, after I die. I'm supposed to grow future leaders to carry on what I've been doing while I'm alive."

"Not just carry on, but even exceed!" The Chaplain said. "Look at what Jesus' followers accomplished since his death and resurrection. There are more than 2 billion Christians in the world today.[8] That's a lot of fruit! If you started counting Jesus' followers out loud, one per second, after 31 years, you would still be less than half way to finishing. And of course that number is still growing."

Traveler said, "And Elisha did twice as many miracles as Elijah. I see. The people you lead and influence, who you leave behind after you die, they bear more fruit than you did yourself while you were alive."

"Exactly," the Chaplain said. "And that group of leaders you grow, they are your leadership team. This is how John chapter 15 works. This is how you bear fruit."

"So how do I disciple my kids? How do I mentor and grow leaders?"

The Chaplain said, "Let's take a look at Jesus' life and see how he grew leaders. Jesus trained his disciples for leadership first by loving them. He was engaged with them, they traveled and lived together for three years. And of course he taught them, sometimes in small groups, sometimes as a part of a greater group. And he also prepared his disciples for leadership by giving them responsibility. Who baptized? Who managed the money? Who passed out the loaves and the fish? Jesus delegated these and other tasks rather than doing them himself. So love your people, engage in their lives. Teach them, provide them with what they need to lead. And look for opportunities to give them responsibility, responsibility that will stretch them and help them grow. Obviously Jesus didn't physically address every one of the 2-plus billion Christians alive today. He started with his disciples,

> *Calling the Twelve to him, he sent them out two by two...*[9]

"And those leaders reproduced other leaders who reproduced others and so on,

> *Therefore go and make disciples of all nations, baptizing them in the name of the Father and of the Son and of the Holy Spirit.*[10]

"Jesus, our master and Lord, bore the ultimate fruit for God's kingdom and provides the ultimate example of leadership."

Traveler said, "So I'm to love them, engage them, teach them, and find ways to give them responsibility."

"Yes, and when you teach, it's usually best to start with strengths," the Chaplain said.

"And correct weaknesses," Traveler said knowingly.

"Sure, but only when necessary. By training people in their talents, and by assigning people to work in their areas of strength, you'll help people to grow and perform the way God designed them to. There's really no better way to motivate people."

Traveler nodded, a look of surprise on his face. He realized he had been trying to "fix" people rather than encouraging them in their strengths.

The Chaplain continued, "As much as you can, create an environment where they're free to take risks. And connect them with people who are successful in their field."

The Chaplain could see that Traveler was getting it. Traveler said, "Growing leaders, encouraging people in their strengths, leaving behind people who will bear more fruit than I have—this whole fruit thing is huge!"

"Yes it is," the Chaplain said. "Now I have to ask, what about Grace? I remember you said you would speak with her before our next meeting. It's been a year. How did it go? How are the two of you doing?"

"I'm trusting her," was all Traveler said.

"Is she still on the internet late at night?"

"Yes."

"Well then, don't you think you need to talk with her?"

"Even if I do have a talk with her, it would have to be next week. I'm leaving town for a few days."

"Traveler, what if this were someone you were responsible for at work? How would you handle it?"

By the look on his face, the Chaplain could see Traveler recognized the truth in the analogy. "I guess I would talk with them, privately."

"Have you ever had to do that before? At work, I mean."

"Well, yes, of course, I have, a number of times. It just seems so much easier at work than it does with Grace, at home."

"Traveler," the Chaplain said gently, "in my experience, when a situation like this one is avoided, it's because of fear."

"Fear? Fear of what?"

"Fear of what might be found."

"That's not it."

"Are you sure?"

"Yeah I'm sure."

Now the Chaplain was silent. He looked at Traveler with his clear calm eyes. He looked for a full ten seconds.

"If the eyes are the windows to the soul," Traveler thought to himself, "mine are the most transparent windows in the world right now." But instead of confessing his fear that Grace was having an affair, he felt himself becoming angry and defensive. Traveler said, "No way. Fear has nothing to do with it." The words blurted out, much faster, and much louder than Traveler had intended.

"You have to confront her Traveler," the Chaplain said firmly.

Traveler was surprised at the power of his own emotions. For the first time he actually felt angry with the Chaplain. He became afraid he might say something he would regret. So he stood up, and walked out.

Your Story

1. How often do you communicate with your family members? With your team at work? With God?

2. Is there anyone you tend to communicate with less than you should?

3. Describe a time when you saw someone take an interest in another person and help them to grow.

4. What is a coaching tree and who has the greatest coaching tree in NFL history?

Grace Face to Face With Her Past

It was Wednesday at 9:00 PM, and Grace found herself seated in a bar.

She didn't normally go to bars and she never intended to go to this one. She went into the bar and grill for a late dinner after an evening Bible study. She hated eating out alone, but she was tired and hungry. Traveler was out of town on business for a few days, and she just didn't have the energy to cook for herself. When she entered the restaurant, they asked if she'd like to be seated in the bar because the service is quicker, and without thinking, she said, yes.

She was escorted to a pub table. As she walked through the familiar place, she noticed it was looking a little run down. Not long ago this was one of the most popular restaurants in town. But tonight the crowd was sparse, even considering the late hour. Recently, a new bar and grill opened nearby. It was obvious, the old hot spot was losing customers because of the new place down the road.

Just about the time her food arrived she felt a tap on her shoulder, it was Ethan Arnold's younger brother, he was seated at the table next to hers. They made idle conversation about high school and old friends for ten or fifteen minutes.

Then in walked Ethan.

"Thanks for the text little brother," Ethan said smiling, as he set his motorcycle helmet on Grace's table and sat down.

Chatting on the social network was one thing, but Grace was completely caught off guard when she saw Ethan face to face. He looked more than a few pounds heavier than he did in his pictures online, but she had to admit, he was still nice looking. He was a few inches taller than Traveler. His face wind burned except for the area around his eyes where his goggles protected. He wore motorcycle leathers.

She remembered their chat session awhile back when he invited her to go for a ride on his motorcycle. She never did take him up on it. "If he asks me tonight," she thought, "it will be much harder to say no."

Your Story

1.   *Describe a time when someone asked you to do something you knew was wrong. How did you handle it?*

Example

Imitate me, just as I also imitate Christ.
—1 Corinthians 11:1 (NKJV)

The next year was one of the most exciting, rewarding, and at the same time, painful years in Traveler's life. At work he was identifying future leaders, training them in their areas of strength, mentoring them, and delegating assignments that would stretch them. He arranged to connect his future leaders with highly successful leaders from both inside and outside his own organization. Sometimes he even grew a leader by assigning that person to grow another leader. As well as things were going with work, Grace's late night internet habit continued to cause him pain. What would have been completely out of character for him professionally, plagued him in his marriage. He just couldn't bring himself to confront her on the issue.

But at work, putting the Chaplain's recent suggestions into practice was having a dramatic effect. Traveler's department had been doing well up to this point, but now it began to soar. Nick was beside himself with professional jealousy and pointed out to Traveler's supervisor the one area he could find a problem with. For all of Traveler's department's success, most of his people had the bad habit of taking extra long lunches and breaks. Traveler knew it was a problem. After he heard from his boss about Nick's complaint, he spoke with his people about it individually, but there was no change. He addressed his department as a group but still no improvement. He cajoled. He persuaded. He even bribed. But nothing seemed to work. He finally recognized it was becoming a distraction so he arranged to talk with the Chaplain about it.

"Traveler! It's been awhile," the Chaplain greeted Traveler warmly.

"How are you?" Traveler asked.

"I'm blessed," the Chaplain replied. "What are we going to talk about today?"

"How about if I start with an apology. I'm sorry I walked out the last time we met. I was way out of line."

"I appreciate that Traveler, but I don't hold it against you. I get it, the hurt, and the emotion you must feel from what's been happening in your marriage. Why don't we pray."

Traveler immediately stood beside the Chaplain and both men prayed together. They thanked God for their reconciliation, they prayed for Grace, they prayed for Traveler's marriage, Traveler thanked God for his success at work. The Chaplain thanked God for his friendship with Traveler. Traveler prayed for the Chaplain's ministry.

After the prayer both men sat down and the Chaplain asked, "So besides Grace, is there anything in particular you'd like to talk about today?"

"Lunches and breaks," Traveler said.

"Interesting topic. How's work going for you in general?"

"Well, I have to thank you for teaching me about that whole fruit thing. I can't believe the difference it's made. I mean, really, I never would have believed it had I not experienced it."

"It's huge," the Chaplain said.

"Yes it is," Traveler replied. "But there's something going on that's bothering me."

Traveler paused, but the Chaplain just looked at him expectantly.

Traveler said, "Since our last visit we have been doing incredibly well. It's just this one thing."

"Lunches and breaks?" the Chaplain asked.

"No, not just lunches and breaks. Well, yes, lunches and breaks, but it's how my people are taking them. They're just sort of leisurely about the whole issue. They tend to take long lunches and long breaks. And no matter what I do or say about it, it doesn't seem to change."

"And they're doing well otherwise?" the Chaplain asked.

"Yes, they're doing great."

"Huh. Let me ask you something, How are you about taking lunches and breaks?"

Traveler swallowed, "My lunches and breaks are a little longer than they should be but…"

"But what?"

"Well, I put in a lot of extra time, to handle all the responsibility I have. I come in early, I leave a little late, I usually work half a day on Saturday. So, if I take a longer break, or a longer lunch, I mean, what does that matter? And you know what? Most of my people are the same. They also come in early and tend to leave late."

The Chaplain smiled, "Traveler, everyone remembers the story of David and Goliath right?"

"Yes."

"But do you remember David's men who are credited in the Bible with killing giants?" the Chaplain asked.

"No."

"Abishai the son of Zeruiah, Sibbechai the Hushathite, Elhanan the son of Jaareoregim, and Jonathan the son of Shimeah, they were all David's men. They all spent time with David. Having spent time with David, they were influenced by David, and they became like David. They became like David, and eventually, like David, they became giant killers. Their life paths led them to the same place as the life path of the leader they followed. You're example to your people is one of the most powerful dimensions of your leadership."[1]

The Chaplain paused then said, "You, are in very large part, the future of the people you lead. Your wife, your children, your employees, the kids you coach in soccer, their life path will almost certainly run through the same neighborhood as yours. This is a daunting principle because we're all flawed, we're all sinners, so we know everyone of us is going to fail at some point. Yet we're commanded,

> *In everything set them an example by doing what is good.*[2]

"Few of us try sushi, social media, or facial hairstyles unless we are introduced to them by a flesh-and-blood model. Humans do not learn to speak, read, write, tie shoes, or perform a vocation without steady doses of imitation"[3]

Traveler said, "You know I just read the other day where Paul the Apostle said, 'Imitate me, just as I also imitate Christ.'"[4]

"Exactly, that's it!" the Chaplain said. "Christ is the key. Besides the simple fellowship God desires you to enjoy with Him, your deep and thorough study of Jesus Christ is for the purpose of growing your ability to imitate, to imitate him, to imitate Jesus. Letting people see Jesus live his life out through you is one of the most important parts of leadership there is."

"Okay, I understand that, and I really try to set a great example, but what about the times when my daughter blows off church, or when she lies about what she watched on TV, or my employee who called in sick when I knew he was at the lake? Sometimes it feels like even when I'm knocking myself out to set an example, nobody's really changing."

"Great question. Let me ask you this, you would agree Jesus set the ultimate example for all of us?" the Chaplain asked.

"Yes, of course."

"Then let's take a look at some of his results in the relative short term. The disciples argued about who would be the greatest in the kingdom.[5] Most of Jesus' disciples abandoned him after the teaching on communion.[6] One of Jesus' disciples betrayed him.[7] The disciples fell asleep twice in the garden of Gethsemane after Jesus asked them to keep watch.[8] And Peter, when he was asked if he was associated with Jesus, cursed, swore, and denied he even knew him.[9] So did Jesus, after experiencing these reactions to his leadership and his perfect example, did he say, 'What's the point? Forget it. I quit?' Of course he didn't. Jesus persevered."

The Chaplain continued, "Jesus recognized he was bearing fruit, and bearing fruit takes time. Bearing fruit involves setbacks. Frosts will come, insect infestations will descend upon the work, droughts will occur, the irrigation system will break. But in spite of the setbacks, have faith. In its season, fruit will be born. Wait for that season."

"So what should I do?" Traveler asked. "About work?"

"How's your example in other areas?" the Chaplain asked.

"You'd really have to ask the people I work with," Traveler said.

"Okay," the Chaplain said. "But if you had to answer, what would you say?"

Traveler looked embarrassed. "I guess it's okay. It's just the lunches and breaks I think. At least that's my perception."

"And you said your department is performing well, right?"

"They're really outstanding."

"Well, if you really want them to shorten their breaks and lunches, then…"

"Shorten mine," Traveler interrupted.

"Yes, shorten yours. For good or for bad, your example is extremely potent. And when your good example doesn't produce results, don't give up.

Remember, bearing fruit takes time. Even Jesus, who loved and led perfectly, faced setbacks when it came to his followers, following his example."

"It's so simple," Traveler said.

The Chaplain said, "Set a great example for those you lead, their future depends on it."

Traveler said, "I'm going to confront Grace."

The Chaplain said, "I know you want to."

The Chaplain looked at Traveler for a few moments, smiling. Traveler sensed there was nothing more to talk about today, maybe even for a long while. They exchanged good-byes, and the Chaplain left Traveler with, "I'll be praying for you Traveler."

<u>Your Story</u>

1.   Who in your life are the most important people for you to set an example for?

2.   What are you doing to set a good example for them?

3.   What more will you do in the future?

The Last Visit

Greater love has no one than this,
that he lay down his life for his friends.
—John 15:13

It had been awhile since he'd seen his friend, the Chaplain. Traveler happened to be driving by his office one day and decided to stop in. For the first time he wanted to pay a visit, not because he was desperately seeking the Chaplain's advice about work, but rather, just to say hello, and also, to make a confession.

"Chaplain!" Traveler greeted the Chaplain with a big smile.

"Traveler, great to see you," the Chaplain returned the greeting. "How have you been?"

"I'm a blessed man," Traveler said simply.

"I'm glad you stopped by," the Chaplain said. "Grace was here just a few days ago."

Traveler felt his stomach knot up instantly. He

thought to himself, "What reason could she possibly have for stopping to talk with the Chaplain?" Besides stopping just to say hello, he intended to confess: he still hadn't braved a confrontation with Grace. He knew he should have, long ago. Could his disregard for the Chaplain's advice have resulted in the destruction of his marriage? Is that what was happening here?

The Chaplain saw the color drain from Traveler's face at the mention of his wife's visit. He quickly added, "She shared something with me, Traveler. She said you would never say anything, but she wanted me to see this." The Chaplain handed Traveler a handwritten note. It took a few moments, but Traveler recognized it.

Traveler,

    Thank you for the time that you spent here leading our department. I know that you always look for the best in everyone. You have helped me to temper my sometimes judgmental nature by watching you deal with difficult situations. I also know you seek to be more like Jesus, and I have to say, I can see Him in you by your honesty, integrity, and love. Those under your leadership as a vice president are truly lucky to be receiving a person such as yourself as their new VP. I hope they appreciate you as much as I do.

Sincerely,
Ab

There was a long awkward pause after Traveler read the note. Then the Chaplain said, "So she told me you were promoted to Vice President."

"Yes, I was. To be honest, I could hardly believe it happened. I really thought Nick had the inside track."

"Congratulations Traveler. I'm not at all surprised. And there's something else too."

Traveler shifted uneasily.

The Chaplain continued, "Grace didn't come just to share that note. She came and confessed something to me. She asked me to tell you about it. I refused of course and told her she had to tell you herself. But she wouldn't budge. She insisted I tell you. If I didn't think it was in the best interest of your marriage I wouldn't do it. But Grace really left me no choice but to tell you."

"Tell me what?"

"She told me she had an internet affair with an old high school friend."

The word *affair* seemed to hang in the air. As soon as it reached his ears, Traveler felt his body tense involuntarily.

The Chaplain said, "She said there was a time when she struggled with your obsession with work, and your desire for control. But then she said she's seen tremendous changes in you. She said you're different now. She said she shared the note from Ab because, she feels the same way he does. She told me she sees Christ in you Traveler."

Traveler, who had been standing, sat down.

The Chaplain said, "She told me she was pouring her heart out to this old friend of hers from high school, on her social network. She shared that he's a he, a man. She said, not long ago, she ran into him at a restaurant while you were out of town. And she said she shut him down. She cut off all contact with him, completely."

After a moment, Traveler asked, "Was there any physical relationship?"

"No, none," the Chaplain said. "It was all messages back and forth on the social network. I've heard some people call that an *e-affair*. I'm not sure what the *e* stands for, electronic affair? An emotional affair? Even though there's not face to face interaction, these things can be very damaging to a marriage, no question. Anyway, in her case, the restaurant was their only face to face meeting. And she ended the friendship right there. She said it was easy to do it, because of you, because of who you've become. And she said she wanted to thank me for my influence on you. Of course you and I both know that's nonsense. I explained to her, it was Jesus Christ who changed your life."

A wave of relief passed through Traveler's body. He really didn't process anything the Chaplain said after he heard the words, "No, none…" He was speechless.

Then the Chaplain said, "I'm not at all sure Grace is ready to share this with you Traveler. If she was, I wouldn't have mentioned it. I think you'd agree, now's the time to finally have that talk with Grace."

Traveler turned his attention back to the conversation, "I know, I know, you're right, of course, I will, I will talk to her. And I should have talked with her about it before. I can see the whole thing is my fault. I was completely consumed with work. For too long I didn't give her anything of myself. And having the talk, of course you're right, it would have been better if I confronted her the way you told me to. But early on you told me, the most important thing I could do to impact any relationship is to change, to become as much like Jesus Christ as I can. That made me realize I really have no control over my wife, or anyone else for that matter. The only person I really have any significant control over is me. So I figured out the most impactful thing I could do for our marriage relationship was to change myself: to become as much like Christ as I could."

"Of course you're absolutely right," the Chaplain said. "What do you think helped you most, to become more Christ-like?"

"I guess it came down to three things mainly: persistently praying for the Holy Spirit, a deep study of Jesus' life, and finally realizing I had to lighten my schedule. For too long I was achieving productivity at the expense of living, and loving, like Jesus."

The Chaplain nodded silently. It was then that Traveler noticed something different about him.

Something had changed. Traveler suddenly saw how much older the Chaplain looked since his last visit. "Wow, his years as a soldier have taken their toll," he thought. But it was more than that. The Chaplain looked as though he was trying to hide something. Then it struck him, it was pain. The Chaplain was in physical pain.

The Chaplain could sense Traveler had seen through his efforts to hide it. "I haven't much time left," the Chaplain said. "I'm going home soon. I have cancer. Those of us who served overseas are more prone."

For a brief moment, Traveler felt cheated and abandoned. "Your time is cut short then," he said with an edge of protest in his voice.

"I don't regret it," the Chaplain said. "It was a great privilege to serve as a soldier." He paused then said, "It's been a great privilege to serve you, Traveler."

The news about his wife, the news about the Chaplain, it was just too much to handle all at once. Traveler had to steel himself, he felt tears start to well up, but he shed none.

The Chaplain said, "I've lived a life that was difficult at times, but difficult isn't necessarily bad.

I've been blessed, very blessed."

"How can you be so calm?" Traveler asked.

"Do you know what success is?" the Chaplain asked back.

"I think you're going to tell me."

"Success is the peace of mind you gain from knowing you did the best you could with the talents God gave you.[1] And of course I enjoy the ultimate peace from knowing I'll be united with Christ."

They sat together in silence for a long time, comfortable with each other.

Finally Traveler stood up and said, "Is there anything I can do?"

"I know your heart, Traveler," the Chaplain said. "I know you want to help, but my family is taking good care of me."

The Chaplain stood. They looked at each other for a long moment. Then Traveler gave him a bear hug and said in a voice choked with emotion, "I'll miss these meetings."

Then he walked out the door.

On his way home he thought about what he would say to Grace. And he thought about the Chaplain. And he thought about this scripture.

> *Greater love has no one than this, that he lay down his life for his friends.*[2]

"That's it," Traveler thought. "If I had to pick one scripture to describe him, that's the one. He lived for others. And he lived for Christ."

Traveler and Grace had a very long conversation that night. It was marked with confession, and tears, and apologies, and smiles. Grace shared everything about her e-affair. Traveler apologized for damaging their relationship by prioritizing work ahead of their marriage. After it was over, all was right with Traveler and his wife Grace, and with his daughter Hope too.

Your Story

1.   Soren Kierkegaard said, "Life can only be understood backwards; but it must be lived forwards." What scripture verse or saying do you want to describe you when your story is over, when you've passed over to the other side? What do you want to be remembered for?

The Master

*...for I came from God and now am here.
I have not come on my own; but He sent me.*
—John 8:42

Traveler had just returned home from the Chaplain's widow where he helped with some yard work and painting. It was late spring, and the weather was perfect for working outdoors. He was still in his work clothes, covered in dirt and paint, when he noticed an ordinary young man approaching his front door.

The young man knocked and Traveler greeted him heartily, "You must be Adam. How good to see you. I understand you have a few questions for me." Adam took a half step back toward the street. He was somewhat taken aback by the bear hug.

"Come in, come in. Sit down. Can I get you anything?" Traveler asked, shutting the door behind them.

"No, I'm fine," Adam said as he sat down.

"How can I help you?"

Adam looked at the floor and answered, "Well, my wife and I have a new baby, he's six months old, and I, well, some friends told me I should come talk with you."

"What would you like to talk about?" Traveler said.

"I guess I just want to be the best dad I can be, but I don't really know how."

"Adam! God bless you for your desire to be a good father. Where would you like to start?"

"I want to know everything!" Adam said, his face suddenly coming to life. "Everything I need to know to become the best dad, and the best man I can. I want to know--today."

"You want to know everything? Today?"

"Yes, right now."

"I'm sure I don't know everything you want to learn. And I'm sure I can't cover everything I do know in one meeting, but I'll do what I can. How about if we open with prayer?"

Traveler led the young man Adam in prayer, asking for the Holy Spirit to move mightily in his life, and during their meeting.

After praying he began to share, "Adam, most people don't recognize, when they become a husband, or a father, they become a leader. The day of your wedding, you became the leader of your family. From this moment on, I want you to think of yourself that way."

"I can do that," Adam said.

"Good," Traveler said grinning. "To become the very best husband and the very best father you can be, and I believe that's exactly what our Father in heaven wants for you, you must become the best leader possible. And Jesus is the key to becoming that person, that person our Father in heaven wants you to become. Sometimes your wife, or your children, or maybe someone at work might make you feel you're inadequate, as a person. I suspect that might be why you're here."

Adam nodded.

For the next hour Traveler shared about Jesus.

How Jesus overcame the doubts and opposition of the established religious authority of His day.[1]

How Jesus was first influenced by our Father in heaven, before Jesus ministered to people here on earth.[2]

How Jesus loved us so much, he gave his life for us.[3] And how his love and commitment to us is precisely what allows him to set the bar high for us.

How Jesus came to serve us, humbly, as he demonstrated when he washed the disciple's feet at the last supper.[4]

How Jesus had a great passion born of the

Holy Spirit.[5]

How Jesus possessed that paradoxical and dynamic combination of great passion and great humility that all truly great leaders exhibit.[6]

Traveler shared how Jesus bore abundant fruit, by growing leaders.[7]

And finally he shared how Jesus set for us the ultimate example, of what a great leader is.[8]

Traveler finished with, "Jesus, our Master and friend, provides the ultimate example of leadership. Adam, if you forget everything else I teach you, remember this: spend time with Jesus, learn about Jesus, go deep in your study of the person of Jesus. Go as deep as you can."

"That's a lot of information," Adam said looking a bit wide eyed. "What's next?"

"Let me pray about that," Traveler said. "Come back next week, and I'll give you an answer."

Your Story

1.   *Who can you help grow as a follower of Jesus Christ?*

About the Author:

Kurt Bennett was born and raised in Chicago, Illinois. He was educated in Rockford College and Eastern Oregon University. He spent most of his professional life as a firefighter. In 2010 he started blogging and writing books. Kurt lives in Oregon with his wife Kathy and his two sons.

For more by Kurt Bennett go to GodRunning.com.

Notes

3. Me, A Leader?
[1] Psalm 75:6-7 (KJV)
[2] Warren Bennis and Burt Nanus, Leaders (Harper and Row, 1985)
[3] 1 Samuel 16:6-10
[4] 1 Samuel 17:28
[5] 1 Samuel 17:33
[6] 1 Samuel 17:42
[7] Genesis 20:2
[8] Exodus 2:14 and 4:10
[9] 2 Kings 2:23
[10] Isaiah 6:5
[11] Job 2:9
[12] Joshua 1:6-7, 9
[13] Acts 8:3
[14] Matthew 16:21-23, John 13:8, John 18:10
[15] John 18:17-26
[16] 2 Samuel 11:2-4; 2 Samuel 12:24
[17] 1 Timothy 4:12

5. Influence
[1] John C. Maxwell, The 21 Irrefutable Laws of Leadership (Nashville, Thomas Nelson, 1998)
[2] Dr. Alvin J. Schmidt, How Christianity Transformed Civilization, (Zondervan, 2004)
[3] Will Durant, Caesar and Christ, The Story of Civilization (Simon and Schuster, 1944)
[4] Acts 4:13
[5] 1 Corinthians 11:1

7. The Greatest of These is Love
[1] Sun Tzu, The Art of War (Hodder and Stoughton, 1995)
[2] Romans 2:4
[3] 1 Corinthians 13:13
[4] 1 Corinthians 13:7

9. Humility
[1] Jim Collins, Good to Great (Harper Collins, 2001)
[2] Psalm 75:6-7 (KJV)
[3] 1 Samuel 30:1-6
[4] 1 Samuel 30:6 (KJV)
[5] Luke 18:9-14
[6] Luke 18:14
[7] Philippians 2:3
[8] 2 Corinthians 4:5
[9] John 13:4-5

11. Passion
[1] Jim Collins, Good to Great (HarperCollins, 2001)
[2] Exodus, Leviticus, Deuteronomy
[3] Numbers 12:3
[4] 1 Samuel 18 and 2 Samuel 23
[5] 2 Samuel 7:18
[6] Philippians 3:13-14 (NKJV)
[7] 2 Corinthians 4:5
[8] Judges 15:14 (KJV)
[9] Online Etymology Dictionary:
http://www.etymonline.com/index.php?term=enthusiasm
[10] Luke 11:13

13. Fruit and the Finer Points
[1] Colossians 3:23 (KJV)
[2] John Maxwell lecture, April 9, 2008
[3] Bill Hybels, Courageous Leadership, (Zondervan, 2002)
[4] Proverbs 11:14
[5] 2 Kings 2-4 (KJV)
[6] John 15:5-8 (KJV)
[5] 2 Kings 2-13 (KJV)
[8] Max Fisher, Our Christian Earth, Washington Post Online, December 18, 2012
[9] Mark 6:7
[10] Matthew 28:19

15. Example
[1] Jon Courson, Jon Courson's Application Commentary—New Testament (Thomas Nelson, 2003)
[2] Titus 2:7
[3] Jason B. Hood, Imitating God in Christ: Recapturing a Biblical Pattern (IVP Academic, 2013)
[4] 1 Corinthians 11:1
[5] Mark 9:33-34
[6] John 6:54-66
[7] Luke 22:48
[8] Matthew 26:38-43
[9] Matthew 26:74

16. The Last Visit
[1] John Wooden, http://www.coachjohnwooden.com/
[2] John 15:3

17. The Master
[1] Matthew 26:1-5; Mark 14:10-11; Luke 22:1-2
[2] John 1:1-2; John 8:28
[3] 1 Corinthians 15:3-4; John 15:13
[4] John 13:4-5; Matthew 11:29
[5] Matthew 3:16
[6] John 13:4-5; Matthew 11:29; John 19
[7] Mark 6:7-12, 13; Matthew 28:19-20
[8] Hebrews 4:15

www.ingramcontent.com/pod-product-compliance
Lightning Source LLC
Chambersburg PA
CBHW020656300426
44112CB00007B/401